UNBECOMING

THE HUGH MACLENNAN POETRY SERIES

Editors: Allan Hepburn and Carolyn Smart

TITLES IN THE SERIES

# Unbecoming

NEIL SURKAN

McGill-Queen's University Press
Montreal & Kingston • London • Chicago

ISBN 978-0-2280-0891-0 (paper)
ISBN 978-0-2280-1024-1 (ePDF)
ISBN 978-0-2280-1025-8 (ePUB)

Legal deposit fourth quarter 2021
Bibliothèque nationale du Québec

Printed in Canada on acid-free paper that is 100% ancient forest free
(100% post-consumer recycled), processed chlorine free

Funded by the Government of Canada    Financé par le gouvernement du Canada        Canada Council for the Arts    Conseil des arts du Canada

We acknowledge the support of the Canada Council for the Arts.

Nous remercions le Conseil des arts du Canada de son soutien.

---

Library and Archives Canada Cataloguing in Publication

Title: Unbecoming / Neil Surkan.

Names: Surkan, Neil, 1989– author.

Series: Hugh MacLennan poetry series.

Description: Series statement: The Hugh MacLennan poetry series

Identifiers: Canadiana (print) 20210262982 | Canadiana (ebook)
20210263016 | ISBN 9780228008910 (softcover) |
ISBN 9780228010241 (PDF) | ISBN 9780228010258 (ePUB)

Subjects: LCGFT: Poetry.

Classification: LCC PS8637.U755 U53 2021 | DDC C811/.6—dc23

---

This book was typeset by Marquis Interscript in 9.5/13 Sabon.

*for Edi*

*The painful love of being*
*permanently unhoused.*
Jack Gilbert

# CONTENTS

III.

IV.

*To be coming apart.*

*To be, coming apart.*

*To becoming, apart.*

*To becoming a part.*

I.

## SOME LIMITS

Just outside Rock Creek,
mist blocks the entire road,
from sky to snow-packed rumble strips,
like a butcher-papered window

behind which everything's draped
in gyprock-dusted plastic, save
a few spackle-humped branches
that, jabbing into view, confirm

I am indeed creeping deeper
into an unfinished room,
which is, far as I can see,
as far as I can tell.

## THE MINIMUM

What is the minimum
required to convey
a landscape, I wonder,
as my father and I drive
from Saskatoon to PA
and all that divides land
from sky is a faint
crease at road's end. Deer eyes
flare, but otherwise
the snow spans evenly
on all sides and it's hard
to say how close we are
to anything but one
another, and so, being
not close, I fix
on lone farmhouses' slight
windows fending off the dusk
like pilot lights. This is where
my father's family re-
started, forty below
on a crude plot, et cetera,
all the pioneer non-
apologies: neo-peasantry,
"not even bootstraps
to pull," become an ethics
of work, survivor's
pride, leisure earned,
and never one
to whine, feelings tucked
like perch under ice
turned isolation in old age, brute

stubbornness, a frail
rage. He refuses
to eat, Dad says. I nod
and watch the mill
slide past, frost glinting
on fresh-stacked timber.

There's no time, my gowned
grandfather grumps, you must get
to work. His blood-logged legs
make the hospital bed
look heaped with twin
barrows. Having decided to die,
he sips less Ovaltine
than would sustain a baby,
drains his body
gradually, a gravity-
flow grain elevator. Yet
still he skeptically recounts
my hands when we play
cribbage on his lap, probes
about my degree, briskly
and bewilderingly concrete,
as if his mind,
crisp as the sifting air
outside, were simply poised
to vault like a chill
into new limbs, keep on
without interruption. Hence
the air in here: forced, and stuffy
as, again and again,
my father asks if he has
"any pain," and my uncles
sprinkle well-wishes
from church and bridge
club till he practically
sparkles with hard granules
of sugar that begin
to burn like salt on ice
when, time to leave,
he won't return
love to any of us.

*

By peeling too many potatoes,
my uncles comfort one
another, whittling
the roots down, snarking
about Grandpa's nurses
who "act like they don't care
he was a doctor"; joke
about the time, collapsed
on the rancher floor,
he yelled, "don't help me up:
show me!" Peel
faster, flexing their feet,
glance up at the chuckling
water on the stove.
They were all raised to be
geodes, pressure-hardened, gleams
immured in the centre,
which was just fine
till now, when, no
matter the russets
scraped, the impressive
leftovers, something
aches, sprouts unruly
eyes, a creeping incoherence,
and endurance, mistaken
for bravery, founders – raw
potatoes forced to soften.

\*

What is the minimum
required to convey
love, I wonder,
as the minister
gestures to the back pew
where my grandfather would wait
listening while my grandmother
practised her accompaniment
on the organ, clacking keys
the colour of tea-stained teeth
that lagged before
sound whinged through
the pipes. Even once her memory
had thinned to a fine sleet,
she'd repeat hymn fragments
on any keys she touched.
My grandfather refused
care, cooped her in the house,
snapped whenever she asked
twice, ten times, pirouetting
on her bleary patch of ice;
or pounded ahead
while she, lost soloist, tripped over
unfamiliar harmonies,
missed the coda
altogether. Lag, bitterness,
overwhelm mislabelled
independence; comfort turned
solvent in which
she vanished – negative
space among
sagged furniture, clouded
glasses. He promptly

followed. Black scuffs
snarl the bowed
linoleum that
makes no sound
as each son crosses
the threshold, looks wildly around
at their absences
whinging between silence.

To be exposed like a perch
shimmering and gaping
helplessly on smudged
newspaper, submitting
to the certainty that the un-
relenting world
vanquishes even perfect
preparations with
lurches, and never
recurs, was impossible
for my grandfather, ice
fisher crouched
over his bore-hole
while flecked streams endlessly
whorled and crossed below.
Now, watching my father mourn,
I try to dip my hands
into the cold, but can't.
Before I'm even aware,
I've walked off the lake
into hoar-frosted firs
sparkling feebly
in still air – line
a tangle of spun
sugar, throat caught
like a broken reel.

\*

My grandparents' ashes
are niched in cubic compartments
of a marble-façaded wall
not far from the mill.
A monocle of ice
spins on the Reflection Pond;
salt burns seam where path meets lawn.
The self-preserving instinct
that brought my grandfather success
had no shut-off, so when
the current changed,
rather than go along,
he thrashed abjectly
against the quickening flow,
which might have been role modelling
via negativa
for his sons, had the instinct
not also been hereditary.
Practical, exacting,
he loved evidently
but never aloud, as clouds
hang like sobs
when the air's too cold
for rain. Or as
an urn contains someone,
but by a wispier name.

\*

What is the minimum
required to convey
shifted ground, I wonder,
as the prop plane shrugs
from a spray of de-
icer. My father sits
two rows away.
At the next terminal,
we separate completely
with predictable words,
but I can feel his generous
fragility –
which I mirror, being
his son, though it doubles
as comfort. I almost
pat his back with a thud.
Instead, the wound
breathes. We breathe
the forced air, split
into the sky.
When I think of my grandfather
on that shabby gurney,
I don't picture his face:
I only see my dad
and his four brothers,
thwarted by permafrost
they're trying to dowse
for water, resorting
to hurling love
on the stubbled, frozen earth.
Then I think of that transfer,
when my father wept on me.

*

The morning my son is born,
dawn spreads like feeling
into numb limbs, and rain
the smell of burnt sugar
soaks the rough remnants
of asphalt in the lane.
All I want to do is love
without impediments;
to live, not survive,
brazenly out of focus,
enough for a horizon line
to thread off in the distance
while we learn to walk
more gingerly,
watching for rivulets
of ants, the squat,
thick-petalled prairie crocus.
I call my dad, share
details – his weight,
his name, how powerful
his mother is –
the minimum
to convey,
amidst dogged relinquishments,
the gravity
of such an appearance,
how much it means
we get to change.

is *No love without threat
of absence*. A fragment,
but nothing's perfect.
And nothing is a verb.

When we met, you sentenced
my other lives to death.
I feared nothing more,
moored to your smallness.

You have my likeness,
but there is nothing
like you. And despite
nothing, you.

Must the fit justify
the factory fire? The puppy
the mill? The cherry
the spray? The calming drive
the frack? The yolk
the coop? The light
the dam? The lifted stain
the bleached reef? The promise ring
the mine collapse? The nonstop flight
the melted ice? The vaccine
the lab rat? The parking lot
the flash flood? The spring water
the bottle raft? The book
the tree? The safety
the freedom? The apology
the theft? The district
the border? The coifed hair
the ozone layer? The cure
the scar? The comfort
the future?
         He wonders,
sitting very still, as the sand twinkles
with timid flies. Freighters slide
into port, their full bladders
and stacked containers
too numerous to hold
in one mind. But his heart
is a hole
that sucks like a whirlpool
and cannot help but grow.

Bungalow after bungalow,

teeth on a saw. Heavy
bag hung from a branch. Mid-

construction Zen pond. Gnomes

lazing on pea gravel
beside a breeze-blocked truck.

Toolshed turned infrared sauna.

And everywhere the wounded
smell of clipped grass. Chemical

defense. Distress signal

to other grass. The kind
of message the receiver

wishes he could do

something about. Guarantee
his own safety. Or help. Poetry

is such a wounded smell.

At best, we feel exhilarated
by our rootedness, and the crude,

whirling blade that moans

in view, that veers without
notice. Till then, feed trough

planted with herbs. River

stones accrued for later. Windsock
swollen with the weather.

Lint pinched then swept around its screen catcher,
what's left of Rae Glacier – old, ash-flecked ice –
keeps scrunching tighter while water,
cold as exposed nerves, clinks through
creased, lichen-tinged scree. It doesn't feel
like the end of the world, and stunted
pines strewn between rocks – no longer
drought-tortured – green in agreement.

But last time I was here, I plucked
a succulent with gable box leaves.
Its single root strand slipped from the shale
how I hope souls flee our bodies.
In a pinch pot on the sill, it died
of too much heaven – or so I
thought then. Now I see the heave
of help given without need.

RESERVOIR

Carp lurk through suburbs
when runoff jumps the dam, sucks
manhole covers up like corks, slops
wallpaper with septic hands.

I mostly keep my body close – rove,
but rarely quit, its cul-de-sacs –
save in, say, a dense flicking
stand of thin birches, their tigered

stalks quivered by the spring
wind, cool light trickling
through the tossing stems.
Then, if lifted, if moved

to swim among the future
sprigs, balled now in burgundy-
armoured buds like tiny
minarets, I see it all

without me – abandoned nests,
old anthill pocks – and am re-
minded that the verb *to be*
gears down but never loses speed

completely. I am not undying,
nor ever pre-bloom, just
a reservoir of energies
that pour in, spool around me, stream

in floods of words that,
like fish scales on furniture,
cling for a while and shine
the dull way dried tears shine.

The leafcutter ant's
cut leaf. Invoice
in the offering
pan. Connect-the-dot
stars, named. Not breezes:
breezeblocks. Hard
water haunting stemware.
Mountain turned
open-faced mine.
The bank, broken. Banks
overflowed. That orca
keeping her calf
afloat. Not music:
score. The splash
as she plunges
away. Handle
on a compost bag. Blood
above the wrong
door. Colour-changing
paint. The softest
case, the hardest
drive. Not dew:
the smell of rain.
The beginning
of owing

you.

*Good Friday, 12 a.m.*

Puzzled by the reversion
to winter, an eggshell tapped
but holding, the river wheezes

and clicks, rephrasing itself
over and over. From the bridge,
I spot a windbreakered boy

showing off by stepping four, five feet on a ledge
of bubbly crust still latched to shore.
Licking index and pinkie tips,

he turns, wets brows with devil horns.
*Come back in!* one voice shrieks.
*Stomp your heel!* another crows.

He doesn't, cornered by his freedom,
and stands there breathing shoals.
Then, crouching, he peers

toward a crack of slithering water –
startles, untangles himself, crawls
back like a shell-shocked scout, getting

there just as the shelf
caves, dunks him to the ribs.
He claws out by stiff fingers, steams

in lamplight while the others
lurk, too thinly dressed, I guess,
to share a coat or touch his skin –

someone offers Amaretto. Now
I see these aren't his friends,
just kids he wants to know. He shivers there,

jeans glazing with rime,
till he's told to go.
As he plods alone through tightly

budded trees, feet punching layered
snow, I hope he arrives, for all their sakes
and, especially, for mine.

Third-generation firs,
planted like barcodes,
repeat, scaly and bald
to their modest tops, where

smoky-green tufts sway.
The ground, needles and salal
around silo-wide stumps,

springs underfoot – or shrugs. No one
comes here save mysterious
harvesters who mark the dead
seedling tips with Campbell's cans,

and a supposed monk
who built a splintery little tower.
She's chanted there for years:

perhaps she feels she's groping
for a keyhole in the dark,
or the dark's a giant throw
she burrows through for comfort.

I flick my headlamp on – the beam
grabs the mottled trunks, bounces
with each step, then widens.

The still symmetry continues,
perfect as two facing mirrors,
till I turn around. Densely
as the multiplying stars above,

red eyes flare and do not blink,
blank, but very aware,
a void of bright stolidity.

I turned the memory in my mind
but it tightened like a screw.
The bay swelled slowly up
the rocks, swallowing

things put on its surface – coins, shells,
dents. Not Orpheus, I knew
I had to wheel and stare
to make it disappear

or heal. I heaved
around, nearly became
tide-stained stone, but at least
part of me survived to look

up. A star that was not
a star slid muskrat-like across
the sparkling depths before,
appearing to dissolve, it hid.

spurted out our clouds
to feel around space like a trapped
bat in an underground
garage. Its image of Ganymede
looks hastily snapped and smudged
with balm. Behind Jupiter,
contact stopped: either *Pioneer 10* drifts
on, teardrop in a cenote,
or it's smashed beyond its name.

We've relinquished control, tried
again, if only to quell
the hunch that in the vast suck
of failed tests and chance events,
someone's relinquished us.

At this sharp
crook in Beaver Point
Road, a cumulus
of blackberries
frizzes with ripe fruit,
veined leaves. Cars slip
past like swallows
in the throat while
three wild horses
tug drupelets
off the spiny
boughs, their wire-
twisting plier lips
tenderly efficient.

On this crisp
July evening,
they're completely
ignoring me. Looking
down, I suddenly notice
the grasses teeming
with baby toads.

II.

AUBADE

Sky a swipe of chalkboard paint,
primer specking through. No shine
this morning: gruffness, dull frost
instead of dew, branches
clawing a tumorous camper
hulked on a truck's bed.
They must have backed it underneath
that Brandon elm with malice –
the fibreglass roof objecting
shrilly as screeched fingernails –
vulgar in their snugness
like rats nested in asbestos. Now,
flushed, flirting, short-lived,
another coal-coloured sunrise brims.

## POETRY WORKSHOP
### WITH MEDICAL STUDENTS

Why are we taking these strands
of words so seriously? they ask,
brows bent like boughs

under the weight of Laura Kasischke,
Who cares what the daughter overheard
her mother say on the phone?

Do you seriously read this alone
and wipe away tears? (There's
a prescription for that.)

Good questions, I mutter, arranging my notes –
sketch of the mom-ghost's tongue, some arrows –
may I ask one in return?

Why are you so invested
in keeping us alive?

and depth
 perception
are pretty
 tight fields
of vision –
 near, far,
an in-between
 that lurches.
In the dim
 gallery, I
tried to
 eye Simon
Starling's *Infest-*
 *ation Piece –*
a replica
 of Moore's *Warrior*
*with Shield*
 that, plunged in
Lake Ontario,
 grew shingly
zebra mussel
 patches – but
she, stooped like
 my dead
grandmother,
 kept standing
in front
 of me, moving
when I moved, so
 close the sculpture

fogged. Her tin
   hair, still
pillow-hollowed,
   glittered with
skin flakes
   as did
her cable-knit
   shoulders, shingly
with invasive
   time. The rest
of the vast,
   nebular room
shied
   from view,
save a lurid
   exit sign.
The sculpture
   has no
face. The ghost
   could not
hear. I
   saw clearly
there's no
   turning back
as – fleshless, a-
   gape – the mussels'
nitid valves,
   like tiny
snap traps
   set off in
a spate
   of chatter,
shut.

BLUFF

Heaving over so her belly,
like a coiled shaving,
arches skyward, the hognose
snake plays dead, tongue lolled,
her stubby tan and brown body
grotesquely warped, as if,
just before you approached,
she quaffed her weight
in bleach. Stay, though, and draw
closer: your stalwart presence
will inspire a second violent
jerk, as, contorting
anew, she dies

again. It says a lot
about us
that you could watch her die
then thrash
then die all day, whereas –
her instinct being proof –
other animals turn
away. Rather than earn
solitude,
her act attracts our faith.

# LATE STYLE

Ruddy salmon struggling up a canyon
front the bulletin. Sprinkled

one or two per pew,
we read the weekly supplication:

Norm, in a coma now;
Anne, who can't remember Pete;

Don, who found his Irene
in the bathroom, on the ground.

Amen. We sponge Christ's body,
broken into even cubes, as juice

drips from the tarnished
chalice. Rising stiffly,

we sing how God draws near
when all feels dark. Voices

squeal outside, from the park.
There are no children here.

A trick of snapping red
cloth, hiding a poised
dagger, their culture
waved the future and they,

furious, ran headlong.
Now we're backpedalling
from the naked shiv.
It was easier for them

to take stabs: they believe
their bodies are vehicles
they'll eject from
to Foreverland.

We're just soft,
coincidental harmonies
buzzing in medias
res, i.e.

the dumps
(which also belong
to them – rubber soles,
feather cushions,

the abundance
of lifetime guarantees
honoured,
then pitched).

## TENT CATERPILLARS

Begun with wisps like melted cling
wrap between branches, a tubed
topmost leaf or two, wounds
gnawed in early fruit, soon

their installation grew
halls, tiers, verandas, vestibules,
till the patchy trees were wound
with their dingleberried

logic: jet-set on credit. Only the good
die hungry. What will be will be
hush moneyed. Keep calm and
half-cut. Buy waterfront.

The pad below a skirt steak
 shrink-wrapped on a foam plate,
  coffee pods with foil tops,
 tape for binding green bananas,
pre-shaven coleslaw bags,
 perforated mustard packets,
  stowed neatly beyond the senses.
  But all we vanished
  persists where blue dozed
 on old maps: a nurdled
vortex, a snaggled
 garbage patch, expands –
  bridging distant continents
  like shaking spit-palmed
  hands. Produce bags
   that drape and glint, bendy
  straws with chewed tips,
 child-proof medicine
someone needed to live.

## DEATH BY A THOUSAND

On the rare occasion I blink
as a scene cuts onscreen,

I'm reminded of the luck
it takes to interrupt

light and return
with continuity, like peeling

an orange down
to pulp and not another

peel – the luck
horror flicks disrupt

whenever someone wakes
glued to the floor, or stitched

inside a bear, or strapped
for pop lobotomy –

every lid-twitch opens
on new life, albeit the same

new life a little
whittled down, whittling to

a sliver over whom
unfamiliars

might one day loom
in shapeless gowns and terrible

white shoes, words blurred
behind their masks

as they prod, cut, and glare
until what's left

is handed back, with the command
to choose: blink or stare.

## FORSAKENNESS

This is the time of year
when the sun goes down at four
and the heavens draw nearer
their inhospitable clarity.

In Krefeld, a fire lantern
wobbled through the sky
then devoured itself
like a resolution, fell

into the zoo's Ape House,
climbing the jungle
gym, immolating occupants
who assumed it would happen,

having already been rescued
from nature reserves
to moulder, picking cuticles,
like botched preserves.

But even they'd have shaken
their too-familiar fists
had they known the lantern
had been lit for a wish.

BOTH

The sun folds itself
behind the Rockies like a man
squeezing through bleachers to grope
for change, peek grimly through
the weathered slats. All day,
Spring had effaced the crusted
snow, exposed a trash
archive, turned each tire track
a sluice. But as the sky mauved,
unfurled a fitted sheet of pewter
blue, I heard the looseness
ratchet shut as brittle
frost stars scaled parked
cars, black-shingled roofs.
When he gets tired,
my grandfather insists his wife's
asleep in the next room,
combines her with
his mother. The cold, climbing, crept
over every fading
thing. He copes by blending
true, untrue: no mind's
a centrifuge. Between
hardened puddles and pebbles
stamped into the road, air –
the line between a fraction –
never ceases its translucent,
amorphous transactions that
make the world look skinned.

My first time here, my father and I
wove through the dusty scree,
hammers and screwdrivers clinking

in cloudy ice-cream buckets.
A friend of a friend of his,
hearing I liked fossils,

had mentioned they could be chipped
from the labile, crumbling ledges.
Among ponderosa saplings

drooped like leather whips,
the first spot I hit
split into key-sized fragments:

every one was stitched
with tiny black leaves. The face
we worked on towered

thirty feet above my father,
thirty-two for me. Peering at the rock,
I imagined my chipping place

as a horizontal plane
where creatures decked in armour
had stamped over these plants

or, better, stooped to graze.
I stood below their ground,
gazing into their landscape.

White Lake, an alkaline pond,
purled dimly in the distance
like a dish of curdled milk.

Its beach, a fringe of coarse sand,
shone with bright soda. Clumped
up to the shore, yellow tufts of thistle

harboured ancient human trash:
a charred farm truck hunkered on its axels;
pinguid, yawning ovens;

a gashed, rotten mattress
spewing stiff coils. The effort
it must have taken to get each item

from the road, across the raking scrub,
lent the place an air of hallowed
excess. As we trudged back

with our finds, the earth crackled
under our shoes – shotgun shells
sun-dulled to pink.

            *


The second time, it was night
and all I could see
was a pallet fire behind shadowy people.

Someone had bungeed speakers
to her quad's rack. Stumbling
on the lumpy

ground, I couldn't locate
the lake, but in the dark the land
looked cleaned. Drunk

on whisky, beer, and boxed wine,
that window where the world
would accept whatever I did

opened. I was dying
to seem brazen. In the crowd,
I ditched Natti and Britt

then spent a half hour
trying to find them.
Three grown men, slouched in bent

lawn chairs, stared like reptiles
at the flames; one turned a buck knife
in his acorn-knuckled hands.

Kisses, cocky scuffling,
soon I was vomiting
against a cool, rough outcropping,

huskily apologizing
to the shifting shale,
till I felt empty

as a crevice. Half images
of someone jumping
through the fire, yelping;

fossils scudding, splashing. No
clue who drove me home.
Next morning, hearing two teens had been

stabbed, I watched my cereal spin, grow
spongy in the bowl, till the flakes
fused thick as clay.

       *

Fifteen years later, White Lake's
a ghostly, wind-mussed puddle
in a radiant basin. By the time

I reach the cliffs, my cuffs
are crumpled up with burrs.
My childhood chisel marks,

like the memory of sobering
at knife wounds on the radio,
have been pattered smooth by rain.

Cluttering the shade, new shards
have split apart, inked
with slivered ferns and ivy:

histories imprinted,
layered, shed, shuffled,
marred. I pocket one for my father

but, walking back, lift
a rusted, wing-shaped piece
of a flattened oil drum

from a snagging cactus thicket
for myself, because, rather than brace,
it broke into something else.

We walked it anyway, though
its stalks were snarled and bent.
Cobs littered the bristled path,
gashed kernels, mouldy chaff,

and fireworks' sooted pistils
jutted among clumps of matted
silk. Repeatedly, we hit dead ends
we could have easily pried

apart but didn't, since
it wasn't ours and, of course,
we'd come that far. Peering round
for where we'd parked, we noticed

in the narrowing dark
the sky had grown a murky skin.
Something snagged your blanket scarf.
We've come this far, I said again.

III.

You dog at a mirror. How
do you glimpse yourself only
when you move? Air
is fertile, all perfumed
motes, pollen,
mould. Do you really feel
desperate, or did
a subwoofer just bloom
over there? Savoury
nausea. Furred everything.
The difference
between me and you?

Me.

with my grandfather meant poaching
from the national park.

His pomelo-sized knees bobbed,
unsteady over black Rockports.

Slinging himself across trees
whose roots had peeled up from the ground

like rusty submarine hatches,
he'd stoop, pluck caps of gold, brown

with petal-thin tope gills. Soon,
the paper bag he held, eye level

for me, rustled vibrantly. No way
would I eat those things, alien

now and soon to be leech-curled
in the pan – especially

since every one I picked myself
was poison: red with curd-white bumps;

grey, oblong, greasy. If anyone
asks what we're doing, he'd say,

we're out for a little walk.
That amazed me: the bag,

so obviously contraband, and yet
we *were* walking. I have no idea

whether he enjoyed my company. I spent
the whole time obsessed

with laws, their infallibility,
how they could be parcelled.

Once, we saw a fox with vole
stuffed in its mouth like a bun.

The pink paws jabbed between faint peeps
which, relatively, were screams.

The fox appraised us carefully
then shoved the body down a hole.

A dryer sheet, whorling among
damp towels in a basement,
infuses the steam
wafting through this Inglewood alleyway.
Cream-thick, cough syrup
and gardenias, the smell
is almost a meal. Most
of a poem is almost.

does not become a consumer.
My son, strapped to my chest,
will not remember this grocery run,

nor tasting this Chilean peach
I'm thumbing for softness. So much
displaces in the realms of produce

and memory. We feel and feel
till someone has to care
for us: I hope he will

visit. We pass the milk, the sweets,
the butcher. All the while
he sleeps, which strangers love, stopping

to simper. I wonder if their snuffles,
their pinching of wrappers,
filter through his dreams, his separate

dark, those ears that match my brother's.
*Subtler, subtler,* beat our hearts
down aisles of cluttered glitz.

# MOLE

I wanted one as a pet
the year I turned nineteen
to say to whichever stoner was over,
*a mole's in there*, and gesture
to a navy plastic tub
heaped with vermiculite and sod.

Now I realize the mole
itself was never required:
the tub-gesture would have been enough –
at least, it was with love.

# IN CELL

On the stem below his mouth,
a sob crouched for so long
it hardened like an aphid
caught in future amber.

Through words tinted by anger,
the sob could oft be seen
but never heard – fragile feelers
and wings that once were green.

# PATHETIC

A chinook arch, like a loose tarp,
lipped across the evening sky
while we were out walking the dog.
Muscling up to a dome of snow,
he shoved his head in past the shoulders,
pulled out something wrapped in foil.

Next morning, it was twelve degrees.
Slush splattered the curb, buds
spangled the trees, crabgrass flexed
in round sun patches. The sudden
heat was so persuasive,

even the river, celery green,
appeared between soft flaps of ice
like remorse on the face
of a forceful denier who,
beholding certain proof, whimpers,
"Human, only human."

And then, as is also human,
clamping down again, the world
reverted, cold as before, except
where, having briefly melted,
it froze harder, and slickened.

## SCRATCHED IN A STALL
## ON THE *SEASONG*

If we can't turn this tanker in the canal
and it's locks from here to the rising sea,
who wants to blow me as the world drowns?

Like a tattoo, their message
jabbed in, rearing
the tender skin

to angry red ridges, but
soon began to itch
and peel – loosely

shingled roof – till
what had been emboldened
sloughed

to its afterimage:
duller, with a few
dropped lines, less

saturated colour,
faded conversation starter,
a blur.

# A FAMILY FRIEND PAINTS
## OUR HOMETOWN

i.

Under long omelette clouds

that liquefy near the tops

of blue-black sage-furred hills,

vineyards grill-mark the land

above the lake whose ripples – if

to scale – would engulf

supertankers whole.

ii.

She omitted the pines, though,
and pickups parked at stuccoed
homes, the Lakeside Hotel's
Parrot Lounge, the Party
Barge (Captain Christano),
the Peach on the Beach slush stand,

and people – there isn't one –
neither humped on ATVs,
nor splayed across the creamy sand,
nor picking in the cherry trees,

as though the landscape only
were worthy of art – golden
boughs, eggy sky, unlit
cliffs accepting night –
or because they're hard to draw,
let alone understand.

iii.

The canvas folds at the Reserve.
I fold: shrug, then wanly gush,
*The mulch between the vines looks very good!*

Though, in such a sunset,
the brown really should be tinged
with daubs the colour of blood.

iv.

*Painting's been my happy place,* she glows,
*since the concussion.*

Sheltered by a boulder arc
that keeps the viscid water a weedy
nursery for suckers,
the marina's docks creak,
crossword on the theme of leisure.
For "Fun" (across, six letters),
I input DENIAL, then,
scrubbing out, try MORTAL,
before settling on CRISIS.
Gasoline ribbons the surface:
a sparkled cigarette boat
trowels past, blue fumes
blurting from its dual props.
Stemming off ILLUSORY
with the clue "More horsepower,"
I faintly pen LONELY
as, from its gull-shat berth,
a pontoon named Fish 'N Chix –
sun-bleached, piled with painted turtles –
glumly nods its jowled head.

*Prince Albert National Park, SK*

At the tail end of my uncle's marriage,
park wardens closed Trapper's Lake.
Outhouses and picnic tables, the trail
from parking lot to shore, were left
to dissolve in the woods, cubes

of sugar on a petri dish. Unfished,
northern pike stocks flourished. Unseen,
loons dove, bobbed, and called. Unloved,
Richard sawed windfall, patched
sheet ply across a bog, stashed
a canoe with dry reeds, then,

cycling in with his paddle, rod,
fished each afternoon alone
in brooding solitude, broken
by clatters of the reel,
the flop of fins on hull.

From endless catches, he'd string
his limit through the gills.
Like a rat king, the placid mass,
bleeding wisps from hook extraction,
dragged half-living in his wake
till the cleaning station, hacked

from lingonberries, nettles, vetch,
glimmered through the birches: metal
table bolted on a hole. There, in swarms
of bold insects, from slimy skins and pronged
white bones, he'd unveil silver fillets.

When the knife first slit in,
stiffening just a little bit,
one in three or four would bleat
a sole terrestrial breath –
the sound of fumbling to make sense
of a new, panging present tense.

*Captain Cook, Kona*

Java finches peer from the glossy
autograph tree while he fills
a faded plastic gazebo
dangling by a dirty cord
with a wide-billed scoop
cut from a gallon jug of milk.
They careen in and jostle,
spraying millet and nyjer seed,
their crisp colours ruffling
so their mite-infested down
and grey, cracked skin cut through
their flashiness, like flames
parting on a garbage pile.
How few pecks each takes
before the feeder's drained again.

# BLUFF (II)

If cornered, a gopher
snake will slip
his slender tail
under a hash of leaves
like a marbled auger,
and quiver
till the raspy layers buzz.
He and a real
rattlesnake may never
meet, and yet
he imitates.

Somewhere out there,
a more potent being
lends his gestures
meaning. That's all
he knows. See
him loaf, belly
full of poached
eggs, perpetually
mistaken.

Word processor
whose writer, face
down on the keys,
dreams of sacred
geometry, the screen
door tingles
with mosquitos
trying to tuck
their wings enough
to enter our RV –
like camels
through needles.

# FAITH

3:30 p.m., rain coming on,
my father and I crawl around, scour
the front lawn for a sprinkler

head tucked somewhere under the grass.
If we don't flag it with red tape,
the plastic casing could get cracked
when he aerates this Friday.

Our knees stain with clippings
as we tousle and part blades, pry
squashed pinecones up like corks,
scatter loamy mushroom caps.

Even as the clouds give and drops
of doubt accumulate,
I cannot stop crawling.

A fused spine of cars
fumes on Centre bridge. Up-road,
a reflective man, enclosed

by orange sawhorses, talks
to an open storm drain,
the grate's rusty ribs

laid on the ashen snow.
No hard hat bubbles
from below. The man pops

nicotine gum, paces his little
corral, murmurs to himself, drags
the grate back into place,

clangs it down,
flumps each sawhorse
on a blinking, curb-cocked truck,

sheds his neon vest,
chuffs,
and lurches toward an alley.

IV.

# NOCTURNE

Cotton swab in an elbow's crook,
a snowman's scalp glints on the lawn,
its body having dribbled off,
scarf sloughed in a flaccid loop.

But now that the mercury's dropped
again, this much at least should keep
catching high beams like the hint
of a word that escapes
me, or maybe doesn't exist.

The moon, fist clenched of blood,
reflects our belated sun,
makes silhouettes of everyone
until they're close enough to smell.

# SHORE

i.

Under a pat of opalescent
jelly, your skin bows

when the Doppler's probe

presses down, foal hoof
at pond's shore. Your heart

laps the room's corners

through the rush-swept speaker, drifts
away as the probe pushes

deeper, now submerged, currents

swirling together. We hold
our breath, until – there:

nimble water treader, a second

heart stirs, faster than yours,
and lighter – yours, but not

for long. The probe

lifts, clicks off, and I,
like an air-strapped skin diver,

rise unwilling with a gasp.

ii.

On the way out, we catch
in the clinic's windows' oily

tint, distorted, as if being

stirred, or crouching through
a wind. The parking lot is still

enough to hear our boots imprint

the snow lit by this early
morning moon's half-swaddled

gleam. We have to care beyond

each other now, and for
however long we get

to live. You have two

heartbeats, and I've a new,
unfurling sense – of our wispy

breaths, fading from view

but not from touch;
of the sounds under silence,

the sounds that shore it up.

After we'd eased
off the highway to
gravel – hush, like dust
on a record needle –
and sagged into wash-out
craters, muffler scuffing
raised culverts, cattle
guards thrumming our teeth,
Max Lake would appear,
slough trimmed with slack
barbed wire and green
cattails: that's where
my dad would park, slanted
in the ditch, and out
I'd scramble, duck the grabby
fence, and wade into weed-
tangled water, clay plumes
blooming under boot, net
poised to scoop newts or nymphs
or, once, a thrashing leopard
frog, so focused that, now
and again, if a cloud
dragged across the sun
to tint the tawny water
shut so I saw myself
wavering there
above the multitudinous
shallows, I'd wait
impatiently
for it to pass.

## STRANGER

There we knelt in the carport.
Grandpa Ed presented me
a dented Folger's can so light
it floated in my hands.

The clear lid, stabbed twice by a fork,
supplely peeled back to waft
sour leaf and coffee breath
from its shady silver depth.

No movement – a tomato shoot
wedged into the sides' grooves.
But on the shiny bottom, curled
around my mirrored eyes,

four green hornworms grimly dozed
like rhinoceros embryos.
Despite a brandished prong on tail,
they looked fragile as shell-less snails.

When I poked one on the head,
it writhed uselessly and bumped
its neighbour, then the next,
until they all were doing their best

impression of stop, drop, and roll,
drumming softly on the tin
like a stranger at the window.
I let them in.

## STRAIN

Colander without holes:
       just another bowl.

       Silence without words:
holes without a colander.

Run in a pilled, dusty shawl, a fire
burns near Oliver,
unravels the sprawled bunchgrass
that swelled with June's abnormal

rains then parched in July's
record heat. Ashes, friable
and frail as moths fumbling
through gnashing day, tremble

on the unbreathable
air, spot sliding doors and glider
wings. In this smudged, grayscale
world, nothing appears:

a caved barn, say,
in a cracked and thistled field
fenced with pines, unpeeled and vaguely linked
like cadaver fingers,

now smoulders to a film
on the roofs of our gaped
mouths. Our throats, blotted, rasp
the harmony of aftermath.

Tobacco, axel grease, aerosol
cologne. Reno garbage
rolly chairs. Saw dust, gyprock, pig
iron shavings. Expired Matco

porn calendar – blondes wielding
nut drivers. Andy, pixelated, sixty percent
burns from the sun kissing leaked gas
while he worked under his truck.

As his wife hosed, down slid
his skin. Marc's three nubbed fingers can still
pinch a zero Phillips, but not
a peeled egg. Larry's cut off

from his kids. "Fucking idiot!"
barked Donn, when Marc threw his back
tweaking a hitch. The Days without Injury Count
reverted. Donn got promoted after he blew

through a blockade at the new ski resort.
Andy whispers Old Donn would come
to in the gravel pit, Charger
teetering over the edge, whereas Larry

rolled a puke-caked mower off Marc
just last weekend. All live
blocks from where they grew up.
All have wives and women they hire.

When Donn told the HR guy
to "stick his nuts up his own ass,"
nothing happened – which isn't
hagiography. Something probably

should have happened, but there's a photo
of the owner's son
curled around the yard toilet –
thumb up, glasses specked with guts –

tacked above the yard toilet. To know Donn
is to love him, says
absolutely no one. No one
knows Donn: it's persona,

I hope. Yesterday, heat-stroked
and dizzy, I placed my hand too close
to a mitre. Donn leapt in. I was
"a cunt hair away from losing it" –

"it" being the Days without Injury Count
and also my hand. See how doubleness
where there should be one
begets a tenderness? I'm talking

about my hand. That same afternoon,
I found a mewling kitten nest
in a rusted diesel heater
right before I fired it up.

Swirling like burnt leaves then settling,
starlings land on merlot vines
planted so close to the highway
diesel plumes and pitched bottles
of piss from hurtling semis
must imbue the tasting notes
the way abused water crystals
look scorched in the microphotos
of Masaru Emoto.

From up here, where the air's
placid and hot enough
that the blotchy rocks emit
a sour vinyl smell, the vines
span all the way to the prison …
Wait: I see now the smell's
that fresh paint on the ledge below –
*Sheena and Pearce* glistering
in the grim sun. Everyone from this valley

knows someone who knew someone
who fell off such a cliff trying
to spray the landscape with their love.
I used to know Sheena.
She'd report her salvia trips in Band.
She sucked at saxophone – never sheathed
her reed. And I'd heard Pearce was gay,
from the same girl who proclaimed
my hair gay, and choir, and pinot gris.

Masaru, did you ever see
your scorched water crystals
scorch others, like people do, in a long cruel chain?
Can the scorched ever be healed?

# DESIRE PATH

Whereas the city's gravel trail
snakes from side to side, nooked
with oversized benches that stick –
layered stain
on stain on spectral
swastikas and heart-trapped names –
this path cuts straight through the wiry grass.
Yet, as is often the case with desire,
it swerves suddenly,
got shy.
Standing now in this stand
of ruddy, felt-tipped branches,
parsing scrub as it wildly
parts, re-parts its hair,
I think how, to get here, someone
had to veer off, followed
by many others, and then all
had to turn back – unless
a few met face to face
and this became a meeting place.

Kneeling in the prow, dusk
thickening, watching for spring

runoff-prized logs
crocodiling the lake-top

while Michael drives us in
to harbour, his speedboat's mineral-skinned

headlight casting a faded,
permeable oval

on the advancing chop:
the bark-coloured water stays

too strange to be breaking
the beam's border, becoming

words from the anonymous
fluid murmuring beyond

the hull. I'm no
sentinel – borders require

effable subjects, and all I see
is flux. Flexing crests,

unknown depths, suddenly
I feel a tremendous

love for my friend
piloting us between

splayed branches, fractured trunks,
as if aided by me

when, really, it's luck.

*

Or crouching on the wharf, steeling
to plunge through ribboned

rhythms. Below, a submerged spring
bubbles crisp tendrils like veins

of quartz. Bobbing like a loose
buoy – faceless, he's swum

so far – Nick wisps
his unmoored voice across

the cupped waves. Language
disperses, spooked school

of smolt, to slivers of void
sound. Diving into colder

skin, I watch my greenish fingers comb
the current till they pierce

ground, its clotted expanse.
This body, mine to hold

down here while it burns
for air and hears

itself, holds
me like a hornet

in a jar. I push toward
the quaking, rucked ceiling, numbed

then kindling outward
as I climb an old aluminum

ladder tethered to the pilings.
These beady limbs – unconstellated,

quick to blur – flicker
when I turn. Nick

sculls gently in.

*

Or leaning over the falls
from a bowed suspension bridge.

Vibrantly churned, a solid
hoared shoot, water congests

the air, padding of wet
decibels accruing in our clothes

till our bodies
cinch to focus, shivering

with excess. It took a while
to notice, but now the weight

slows my movements –
"like you're wearing an amphibian,"

Karl grins, hair plastered over
ears. Stepping into the sun, he begins

to steam – another interruption
of light, fragment

with softened edge, how
I feel (in language).

We turn downstream
from the crush, where the river

slips under a pinch-
point that, somehow, grips

a boulder twenty feet in the air
as if hurled from the sky.

Wedged there, it's begun to grow
a moss meadow. Love spreads

on such impossible rock.

\*

(Coda)

Or your body, mine to hold
sometimes, even when it's sick,

or stippled with cold, or streaked
with crying, or sour

with fear, invisible
but there in the dark. I've heard

your stomach growl. I've heard sharp
breaths as we waded

through streams. The splat
of creek on purple stones

when you wrung out your hair.
Plaster-dry seaweed crunching

underfoot, along the water-
line. We notice

when words mistranslate
to touch, share

friendships, their queer
tenderness, their limits: islands

in lakes in islands
in the motley ocean. We rasp

up gravel shores, drift
into the murky distance,

berth again – anchorless, buoyant.

*

## UNBECOMING

Night advances like molasses,
creeping over the carton-white
mountains. Next to this foreclosed
casino, a dormant bog shallow

breathes. Mealy ornamental apples
snick in spindly, frost-shocked trees
potted around the patio.
Across the valley, a last worker exits

the quarry, headlights glowing between
shale piles like a skull
placed on a candle. We're due
for some luminous thinking –

this very early snow and all –
but why plan when you can gamble?
There's only one guarantee:
nests naked without leaves,

vomit on the paving stones,
the world appears, exceeds, and un-
becomes too quickly for certainty,
just enough for love

to burn, burn with cold,
then go so numb –
blackening toe
we'll salvage or cut tomorrow.

# NOTES

The opening epigraph is from "How to Love the Dead" from *Collected Poems* by Jack Gilbert, copyright © 2012 by Jack Gilbert. Used by permission of Alfred A. Knopf, an imprint of the Knopf Doubleday Publishing Group, a division of Penguin Random House LLC. All rights reserved.

"The Minimum" was inspired by a conversation with the artist and physician Cam Matamoros. It is dedicated to the memory of my grandfather, Metro Surkan.

"Infinities" riffs on James Wright's poem "A Blessing."

"Poetry Workshop with Medical Students" refers to Laura Kasischke's poem "The Eavesdropper, or What I Thought I Heard My Mother Talking About on the Phone, in Another Room, Thirty-Six Years Ago."

"Forsakenness" is after Elizabeth Bishop's "The Armadillo."

"The Infinite Replies" is after Charles Simic's "The Infinite."

The title "Pond Life" was inspired by Lorrie Moore's short story "Community Life."

## ACKNOWLEDGMENTS

Most of this book was written on the traditional territories of the Blackfoot Confederacy (Siksika, Kainai, Piikani), the Tsuut'ina, the Îyâxe Nakoda Nations, and the Métis Nation (Region 3). I feel honoured to live and work on this land.

Carolyn Smart: I'm so grateful for your careful edits. It has been a privilege to work on another manuscript with you. To everyone at McGill-Queen's University Press: thank you for believing in this book.

Earlier versions of many of these poems appeared in *Canadian Literature*, *Cypress: A Poetry Journal*, *The Fiddlehead*, *The Literary Review of Canada*, *Prairie Fire*, *PRISM International*, *Riddle Fence*, *THIS Magazine*, and *Untethered*. Thank you to the editors for supporting my work. Some of these poems also appeared in a chapbook, *Their Queer Tenderness*, published by Knife Fork Book: thank you, Kirby, for your support, mentorship, and friendship.

Thank you to André Babyn, Mikka Jacobsen, Jessie Jones, Larissa Lai, Noor Naga, Libby Osler, Laura Ritland, and Vange Holtz-Schramek for edits, conversations, encouragement, and inspiration.

Thank you to Amy and Steve for providing the perfect writing space at just the right time.

Thank you to Jess, Ian, and Emma for sharing your studio with me (and Lloyd) those early winter mornings.

Mom and Dad: thanks for your generosity and care.

All my love, Luca: first, second, millionth reader; joy chooser.

Edi: whenever you start reading, this is for you.